HOW TO WRITE YOUR MEMOIRS

A GUIDE AND WORKBOOK
BY
AWARD WINNING NOVELIST
JOHNNY RAY

COPYWRITE 2010 BY JOHNNY RAY

PUBLISHED BY
SIR JOHN PUBLISHING

All rights are reserved by Johnny Ray and no part of this guide or workbook can be reproduced in any form without the written consent of Johnny Ray with the exception of the personal use in writing the memoir of the purchaser of this book. Also, these worksheets can be shared with an attorney to discuss legal ramifications of writing a memoir and it can be shared with a memoir ghostwriter in creating the memoir.

Johnny Ray is not an attorney and does not give legal advice. As mentioned several times in the book a competent attorney should be hired to discuss any legal questions you have.

By using this guide and workbook the reader agrees and understands that no warranty or guaranteed is given that your book will become a best seller or, in fact, that you will be able to sell you work to any publisher or obtain an agent. This is the harsh competitive reality of the publishing world. Johnny Ray assumes no liability in any form in you using this book to produce your memoir. Your work is your work and your work alone. Naturally Johnny Ray wishes you the best in writing your memoirs and hopes this guide and workbook will lead you to undertaking and completing this adventure.

OUTLINE

1. INTRODUCTION TO MEMOIRS—WHAT THEY ARE AND WHAT THEY ARE NOT

2. GETTING STARTED

3. REFLECTION ON MEMORIES HIDDEN IN THE CORNERS OF YOUR MIND

4. DETERMINING THE TURNING POINTS IN YOUR LIFE

5. HOW TO STAY FOCUSED ON THE MAIN STORYLINE

6. DECIDING WHICH CHARACTERS TO INCLUDE OR EXCLUDE

7. DOING RESEARCH AND FACT CHECKING

8. DETERMINING THE AUTHORS VOICE AND POINT OF VIEW

9. DETERMINING IF THE BOOK SHOULD BE FACTUAL OR FICTIONAL

10. WHAT IS THE PURPOSE IN TELLING YOUR STORY THAT MUST BE TOLD?

11. DETERMINING WHO THE INTENDED READER IS

12. HOW OPEN DOES THE AUTHOR WISH TO BE?

13. SHOWING VERSUS TELLING THE STORY

14. HOW TO POLISH THE MEMOIR

15. HOW TO FIND AN AGENT OR PUBLISHER

16. OTHER METHODS OF GETTING PUBLISHED

17. HOW TO HIRE A GHOSTWRITER

18. A LIST OF QUESTIONS THE GHOSTWRITER WILL USUALLY ASK

JOHNNY RAY
INTRODUCTIONS TO MEMOIRS WHAT THEY ARE AND WHAT THEY ARE NOT

Memoirs are by basic definition a recounting of one's life, usually the author. The memoir can cover a very short period of that life to a very long period. If the work coves the entire life it is usually considered more of an autobiography. Most of the time the story is told in the words of the author and in first person singular, meaning the use of I said instead of he or she said.

The word memoir comes from the French word *memoire* meaning *memoire* or memory which came from the Latin word *memoria.* It is a personal observation of related experiences recorded in history. A memoir is most commonly about the author's role in historical events either actively participating or observing. Sometimes the author describes the events and sometimes the author will interpret the events so that others know the feelings and emotions of the time.

A memoir is often a nonfiction work of literature as opposed to a fiction where the story is fabricated. However, sometimes it can be written as a piece of fiction and based on a true life story. With that said, many variation can exist between with is true and with is not. A memoir is generally much shorter than an autobiography and covers specific segments of a person's life which are usually important to the central theme of the memoir. Memoirs generally have a purpose, a goal to be accomplished from sharing one's life experiences. However, sometimes, a legacy is what the story teller wants to pass on to future generations.

Since a memoir is very personal to the author, the emotions can be extremely high and sensitive. Coming from the first person point of view the characters and settings can be much more vivid with conflict and emotions more pronounced. The voice must be established to accent the actual time period and location of the story. All of this adds to the one element that draws in the readers—they get to feel the story and live it with the author. Readers love to have a main character they can pull for, especially an author they know who has lived through a crisis or changed the world with their works. In a memoir the author relays events in life as remembered which can be the truth or the way remembered. Everyone perceives events differently and wants to tell their story in their own way. What is significant to one person may go unnoticed by someone else. In authoring a memoir certain events stand out that the author thinks must be told and must be remembered. The older one grows the more they can see that history repeats itself and the wisdom of those living through it can help those without receiving such lessons in person.

So simply stated a memoir is a rehashing of the author's life events as the author wants to tell them and according to what message or goal the author wants to tell. If the purpose is to entertain it would be told much different than if the goal was to instruct or give guidance to a future generation. Consider a memoir your grandparents never wrote but one you would like to read. By changing perspectives like this it helps to understand as a memoirist that to have someone spend time reading your work it has to be interesting and important to them. What one person learns others can benefit from. You do not have to be rich and famous to write your memoirs; you only have to be entertaining. What a memoirist decided to pass on as a legacy is strictly personal.

Determining what should go into a memoir is completely up to the author. The painful moments in one's past one person will want to share with others while another author would never disclose. Some author will want to cover many details and others only a few. A memoir can be close to a full autobiography in length or as short as an *obituary*. This brings us to one major consideration: Most people I think would rather tell their own story than have someone else write a few words posted in the obituary column. The story that must be told can only be told by one person—the person who lived that life and experienced it firsthand.

Yes, the author tells the story, but it can be written by someone else, usually a ghostwriter. In loving memory a storyteller can tell the life of a spouse for example. Or, it could be another person who the storyteller knows well. In any case, the story has to be about a life that has something to tell, something to give future generations. The memoir is the way to preserve this life and pass on a legacy that must be shared.

EXERCISE 1

Since an autobiography spans an entire life and a memoir is a much more workable format for many people, what would you call this slice of life you want to work on? A working title can always be changed later.

_____
_____
_____

Now the hard part, why did you select that title?

_____
_____
_____
_____
_____
_____
_____
_____
_____
_____
_____
_____
_____
_____
_____

It is always good to give a memoir you own definition which will keep you on track with what you hope to accomplish. So, what do you think a memoir is and is not?

JOHNNY RAY

GETTING STARTED

Getting started on any project is always the hardest part. Authoring your memoir is no different. Start with a simple notebook and make yourself notes on what you will need. And before you start doing research which can take forever and be very unproductive ask yourself some questions such as who the intended readers of your memoirs are. The targeted audience is important in knowing how to focus your efforts. Next see if you can give your memoir some basic goals as to what you want to accomplish. Answering the why you have to tell this story adds to your energy to complete the project. Your memories were built over a life time and telling it is not something that will happen overnight.

After creating a purpose behind the memoir concentrate on life events that have made a difference in your life. What are the major turning points in your life? What did you learn the hard way you want others to not have to struggle with? Perhaps you want to leave a legacy and describe how you built your fortunes from your bootstraps, landing in America as a foreigner, maybe not even speaking English so many years ago. Well, I think you get the point.

Considering the method you want to tell the story

adds another dimension. It could be told in chronological order by someone else observing you or in your own words in first person. The story can be told as an accurate accounting of your life or your story can be told in the form of a novel based on your life. This is a good time to think of the impact of the novel on others in your life. Who would you want to include or exclude from you story?

A memoir has a beginning and an end which you can decide on. This gives much flexibility in controlling which parts of your life you want to disclose. These are also the two parts of most stories the reader remembers so you need to make them standout. By clarifying your time frame you do not spend endless hours doing research you will not need.

Before doing the research it helps to make notes on what kind of research you need to do. Remember one important fact here. This is your memoir, built from you memories of how things happened and not a research paper. This needs to be repeated. Research will kill many projects since it is a never ending process. It is also not what the readers are interested in the most. The reader wants to know your feelings and emotions during your life.

By doing the above you will be building the basic premise of your memoir. It can stay flexible due to memories that come to you later but gives you an overall blueprint of your project. It takes some time to put this in a written form but is worth it. If you work with a ghostwriter this will be the first part of what he will ask you to do. Yes, he can lead you through this but the more time he has to spend doing this for you the more he has to charge.

Remember, you are the author, the memoirist of the story. The writer is the person who takes your story and brings it to life using the proper words and writing craft he has learned. You will be a team and the more cooperation between the two the better the end product. Again, there is no reason you cannot do your own writing. For now, concentrate on getting started on your story that must be told.

EXERCISE 2
Why do you want to write a memoir?

_____
_____
_____
_____
_____
_____
_____
_____
_____
_____
_____
_____
_____
_____
_____
_____
_____
_____

What do you see as the main purpose of writing your memoir?

_____
_____
_____
_____
_____

What is it you would like to be remembered for the most?

What do you consider to be your legacy?

Why do you feel like you have the story that must be told?

Have you already selected your slice of life you want to tell? If so, why this one turning point in your life?

Who would you like to include or exclude from your memoir and why?

What amount of time do you have to devote to your project? What will be your working schedule?

How do you plan to do your research?

After collecting all of your material and producing a rough draft, do you plan to write the memoir yourself or hire a ghostwriter? And if you write it yourself, how do you plan to hone your craft of writing?

HOW TO RECALL YOUR MEMORIES
THE PAGES OF YOUR LIFE

There are many ways to trigger your memories but all of them require concentration and a way to record them. One memory has a way to trigger another memory and another. Notes will help you add to them. In brainstorming you want to add as many topics as you can and then edit them later or add others you want to expand on.

You never know where one memory will lead which is fantastic. A small clue here and a forgotten photo there all add up. While adding details, do not forget emotions and feelings of previous moments in your life. At this point do not worry about getting your life in any kind of order. Simply allow memories to flow to you and record them. Searching through old photos can be a fun way to bring back memories. While looking at the photos try to add notes about the photos and leave yourself questions you want to follow up on later. A quick story line can be invaluable in building your memoir.

While completing your memory search make a list of people you would like to talk to or interview later. This could be old classmates, friends and people you worked with earlier. Pay particular attention to those who had an impact on your life and added to turning points in your life. Record any special quotes you remember these people saying. Writing a memoir is much like being a storyteller in olden days. Who around you told stories you remember? Who would you want to pass these stories on to later?

Check old magazines you might have saved for news about what was happening in your life. Find your old yearbooks from high school and college. Old letters you saved can always add special meaning to your life. Perhaps you are holding on to old valentine cards. The sentimental value you maintained in them might need to be shared with others.

Check to see if you have an old personal phone book or address book. Old names will spark memories you may have forgotten many years ago. Using the telephone company phone book search through the business section, who do you know that was an accountant, an attorney, etc? Add the names to your list.

Look on your walls of your home. Old photos will take on a new meaning as well as trophies and awards you won. Think about what were the highlights in your life. What are you most proud of?

Don't forget the social clubs you belonged to. What sports did you love to participate in? Who did you enjoy playing against the most? What was your biggest victory? Can you describe the agony of defeat you felt when you were beaten at your favorite sport?

Concentrate on your senses like smell, sight, hearing and touching and a wealth of memories will return to you. For example what is the best smelling food you ever smelled? What was the best music you ever listened to?

Of course, do not forget the internet. You can find out so much about your family history on line. It can also be a great way to spark you memory. Keep building your list of important moments in your life.

Another technique used by detectives and writers is a storyboard. By adding photos and comments to it, it comes alive and lets you add to it as your memory recalls important data. Recording your memoirs is a way of passing on experiences but also a way of educating and providing knowledge to a future generation. It is not always about being famous, but being important in helping others.

Looking backwards ask yourself what you wish you knew about your parents, their parents and their parents. What do you wish they had recorded for prosperity? What legacy could they have created in a simple memoir? Next, look forward and ask your children or grandchildren what they really want to know about your past. The question might surprise you and will always bring back memories that you need to write about.

In the process of brainstorming allow yourself the freedom to write at will without fear of anyone seeing what you write. Tackle the things that bother you and keep you up late at night. If you have feeling of hate or rejection to love and honor, write them down, your emotions are what will makes a good memoir. Give your point of view, the only one to see the confessional is you. When you think you have it all worked out in your mind, go back and elaborate and write some more about your past. It is time to get deep inside your head and divulge your deepest secrets and fantasies. Trust me it can be very enlightening.

EXERCISE 3

Describe how you will keep up with your notes in building your memoir. Many people use a computer, but a loose leaf notebook works wonders also.

Gather every photo you can find that has you or something about your past. Make notes below on what memories they bring back to you. Rediscover what your life was all about. Focus on what you think should be in your memoir.

Make a list of people you need to talk to and perhaps interview to help you recall events you want to include in your memoir.

Now, check your old phone books for additional names.

HOW TO WRITE YOUR MEMOIRS

Check the walls for old awards you won or accomplishments you made and add to the list below.

The internet can be your biggest friend. Start building key words you need to search and add book marks on places you need to return to.

Do you have old file cabinets with important papers you save? Browse through them and let the memories come back to you as to why you kept them. Be sure to record your memories as you have them so they will not be lost.

_____
_____
_____
_____
_____
_____
_____
_____
_____
_____
_____
_____

Now it is time to record memories from your deep feelings and senses. For example what is the most beautiful thing you ever saw? The best smell you ever witness? The best sound? I think you understand? Record them as you think of these.

_____
_____
_____
_____
_____
_____
_____
_____
_____
_____
_____
_____

Now it is time to dig deeper. When did you feel the happiest in your life, and when did you hurt the most? Recalling the good and the bad adds depth to a memoir.

_____
_____
_____
_____
_____
_____
_____
_____
_____
_____
_____
_____
_____
_____
_____
_____
_____
_____
_____
_____
_____
_____
_____
_____
_____
_____
_____

Not only is it good to make notes of events in your life, but make notes on where you can go to do further research. Where else should you do research?

THE MAIN TURNING POINTS IN YOUR LIFE

Think about the major events in your life and like many people you will remember the obvious birth dates of those around you and naturally your own. But add the times you fell in love, married, divorced, remarried, or simply lived together with a soul mate. Add to these the relationships of your children and their relationships and your world explodes with people affecting your life.

Do not forget your education, the first day in school, the day you graduated or the day you quit. Consider the specialized knowledge you obtain in your schooling. What did you learn you need to pass on to others?

Working various jobs can be interesting. Many people want to know how you started doing what you do. Memories of this can bring back vivid thoughts of what you had to go through. How did you get your first job? What did you learn from it? Did it advance your career or fizzle? Who helped you when you started your career, perhaps a mentor you owe it all to?

How has your health been over your life? If you have never been sick, many people would want to know your secrets for recovery. If you suffered a major illness or accident you will find many people wanting to know how you coped with your problems.

Do not forget your setting. Have you traveled or relocated. What was it like back in the old country? How were you treated when you arrived at a new place to live?

While building your turning points do not think of just events in your life but the emotional impact as well. This is what the reader really wants to know. For example, they do not want to know you simple married. They want to know how you fell in love, how you felt when you approached your wedding day.

Slowly by examining the major events in your life you will see an emerging theme to your work and be able to answer the why question. Yes, the why this story must be told? What events changed you forever? If someone could have warned you earlier in your life, what do you wish they had told you? What words of wisdom or inspiration do you wish you had received?

Should you tell future generation to go for their dream and never give up until they reach it? Or, should you tell them that reaching for one goal may make you lose sight of the small things that are in truth much more important? Perhaps it could be how no matter what life throws your way you can overcome any obstacle.

Hopefully in doing the soul searching and organizing your life your central turning points will emerge. This is a time when a good ghostwriter can help tremendously. By knowing the major turning points the story can come alive. This is when the story shifts form a series of events to a compelling story.

Concentrate on not only the good but the bad in your life. It is the balance that adds to the conflict and the feeling of a life worth following. The pacing of a story makes it interesting and worth reading about. Everyone has their ups and downs. Give the reader reasons to pull for you and to encourage you on. Soon, you will know what those turning points are that changed your life forever and have the basic building blocks to tell your story.

EXERCISE 4

Establishing a time line is important. Arrange these in order later, but record the date of birth and death if important to you of all of those close to you and important to your story.

Education is a lifelong quest. Record the dates and places you learned anything.

Most of us work many jobs over our lifetime. Record the various jobs you held and notes about the time place and events surrounding them.

HOW TO WRITE YOUR MEMOIRS

Major relationships in your life are usually marked with events such as a wedding, etc. Who were the major people in your life and who influenced you? Be sure to add a time line with this.

Health issues play a major role in many people's lives. When has health played a role you need to include in you memoir?

_____
_____
_____
_____
_____
_____
_____
_____
_____

Now to finish up your time line and make sure you add all of the major points on it. What are the other major dates that have affected you and why?

HOW TO WRITE YOUR MEMOIRS

HOW TO STAY FOCUSED ON THE MAIN STORY

Mark Twain once said great novels are created by not what is included but by what is left out. In the process of creating the memoir, the author and writer need to know all of the background and subtle side stories, but have to use judgment as to what needs to be included in the story. This, of course, means much of the hard work has to be thrown out.

Determining what are the major turning points in life can be work but worth it. By concentrating on those times they can be brought to life with all of the feelings and emotions existing then. The special scenes that replay in our minds filled with joys and pains add much more to a story than a factual accounting of events.

So, how do all of the events in a life get narrowed to those special turning moments? There are several methods available. First isolate a time period that is most important to you. It could be your early childhood, or your retirement years. And, of course, it could be anything in between. What molded your life? It could be a certain place you live, a special job you accepted and excelled in or maybe failed in. You could concentrate on an award or trophy you won or write about how you lost everything.

Many people have someone special in their life. While the relationship was intended to last forever, life is not always fair. However life is an adventure and when one chapter of life ends another often opens. Life could be a spiritual journey or what is known as a hero's journey. A memoir is different from an autobiography in that it covers these slices of life and focuses on them, revealing an inner soul that grabs the reader's heart and mind. The reader wants to feel you emotions and enter your world to escape from their own and to learn from your experiences.

While the memoir can specify one particular time, it can also cover several related time periods. Defining what time period to concentrate on is very important to staying on track.

You need to ask yourself continuously if this information moves the story forward and is it a part of the message you want to present to the reader. By focusing on the theme and the purpose for the memoir it gives impact and meaning to the reader. By concentrating on one point the author can present the full range of feelings and emotions associated with that event.

Focus on what it was about an event that changed you for the better or the worst. Why was it so important to you and why is it important to tell others about it? Ask often what it is you really want to say. What lesson did you learn you think others should know?

Sometimes it takes being the devil's advocate and asking what are you trying to say and why should I care. What is in it for me? Why should I be concerned? Connecting with the reader will make them listen to your story and learn about your legacy.

Exercise 5
Focusing your effort is important. Which major events do you want to focus on and why?

Which event in your life do you want to exclude and why?

HOW TO WRITE YOUR MEMOIRS

DECIDING WHICH CHARACTERS TO INCLUDE OR EXCLUDE

Almost no one is an island. Everyone is in contact with people who have a role in their lives. Some people affect their lives more than others and these are the ones that need to be included. But deciding who to include is much more complicated when you look at it closer.

When a person authors their memoirs not only is their story on public display but their friends, family and acquaintances. Everyone has different comfort levels on what they want to share. Everyone has different opinions on every subject. Some people you will make happy others you could make mad.

Sharing the story of others is a balancing act of telling the truth sometimes and working to avoid hurting someone's feelings, not to mention avoiding a lawsuit in the process. Trying to reach this balance requires work and patience. The reader needs to know enough about the other characters to relate to them in the story and feel like the main character is actually living this life in the story.

A problem in adding too many details about other characters is the danger of sidetracking the story and getting off the main message the author wants to send to the reader. The secondary character need to move the story forward and not tie up the words with day to day activities. Also adding too much information on secondary characters is where many authors get in trouble telling things theses character would rather not disclose to the world.

In the first draft many of these details can be added to give a feeling of covering all of the major points. It is often in the polishing that many irrelevant points can be eliminated. Many times there are things the author needs to know but is not important to the reader later.

In including other characters it is interesting to add their point of view and the way they talk. However switching to their point of view can be tricky. It is important to let the reader know whose voice the words are coming from. In any one scene it is best to stay in only one point of view at a time. There will be more on this later.

While adding other characters it is easy to not disclose certain characteristic about them that is taking for granted by the author but completely unknown by the reader. A fully developed character sketch will usually help in adding depth to the characters. The reader needs to be able to picture the character in his mind, not only physically but mentally as to what makes him or her tick.

When writing a work of fiction the names are very important. You want to create a fictional name that brings this person to life. It has to match the sex, time era and ethnicity of the person. The educational background and type of employment will affect the way he or she speaks. Their outlook on life can be forged by their marital status, children, and well as their own life events. It is great to include their own quirky thoughts on life and way of approaching problems. Do they have a unique and strange laugh? Do they have a temper? What is it about this person that annoys you or makes you happy? Do you know their deep secrets, their fantasies? You have to be carefully here in not disclosing too much, but it does help to bring the character to life.

If you are not entering a characters point of view and his or her mind, the way to display their thoughts is with their actions. Rather than saying he stayed mad and angry show it by him hitting things or yelling. The actions of the character reveal everything the main character, which is you, wants to tell the reader.

One of the great advantages of writing characters in a memoir is that the characters are real people that the author knows well instead of the imaginary people a fiction writer has to build every detail out of his imagination. In fact many fiction writers have to rely on someone they know close to their imaginary character to be able to build the profile.

The rub in many cases comes from the reader wanting to know all of the deep secrets of the memoir author and the need of the author to protect some deep personal information. This is a delicate balancing act with many repercussions. There may be people in your life you want to protect and there may be others you would like to destroy. In both cases move slowly and evaluate what could happen. I'm no lawyer but in some cases you might want the opinion of an attorney before you release your memoir. Also, this is another reason you might want to release your memoir in the form of a novel, a fictional piece of work.

One case that I read about involved a writer being sued for writing a novel based on what one person said was his life. He said he was defamed. He also said the author did not get many parts of the story correct. The judge had a fun time throwing this one out of court, but still the poor author had to hire a lawyer and spend time and effort in clearing his good name.

In the end it is much like the lyrics of Rick Nelson in his song GARDEN PARTY where he sang, "you can't please everyone, you have to please yourself." However, the important item to remember, these are secondary characters and your memoir is about you, even if you decide to publish it in the form of a fictional novel based upon your life. Again, this brings up the question of who you want to write the work for. It could be a simple way of recording your life for your family. Or, it could be written for the masses to see.

Exercise 6
Who are the people you would definitely want to include in your memoir and why?

Who are the people you definitely will not include in your memoir and why?

HOW TO WRITE YOUR MEMOIRS

On each person you want to include build a brief character sketch of them so that the reader can actually see them. Remember you know them well but the reader does not but wants to.

HOW TO WRITE YOUR MEMOIRS

DOING RESEARCH AND FACT CHECKING

To tell the truth or to fabricate—that is the question. Sounds simple, but far from it as the real effort begins in a project. Memoirs in general are expected to be totally accurate and truthful. However, knowledge has a way of being slanted over time. Research can build a case for whatever you want to present. What one person considers the truth; another will call it a big fat lie.

If a memoir is based on memories and nothing more, than the truth is what that person remembers and nothing else. If the story is based on research, it is based on the information collected and interpreted by the researcher. The work can state facts or opinions. Another consideration is the intent of the writer. If to publicly embarrass another the work will be looked at differently than to set the record straight.

Research can be fantastic in defending your work, but also devastating if used improperly. The research can be time consuming and in many cases ruin a good story. The story comes from the memories of how things were not so much how they actually were. I know some people will argue on this. But, this is a memoir and not a history book.

Fact checking after the book is written can bring up many points that can cause the book to be rewritten. This can add interesting sidelines to the book or help in the polishing of the story. A fact checker can be the author or another testing for authenticity of the book.

In wanting to make a book interesting or inspiring it is easy to stretch the truth or make the book more sexy or thrilling than life really was. Keeping the authors unique and special perspective on a work is what makes the book come alive. Adding reflections and opinions by the author adds the truth many readers really want to read about. Not so much truth in facts, but truth in allowing people to read your mind, your personal opinions. The reader wants to relate to the author and share the emotions and tugs of war they feel.

Telling the reader up front that the work is a factual memoir or a reflection goes a long way. Building a novel as a work of fiction adds a different dimension. With the amount of truth and fiction varying from book to book, the memoir, a story based on a true life, can appeal to both insiders and the general public. Only the silent brother now in prison, or the unfaithful wife, will know it is them. Exactly how you want to author your memoir, your story is up to you and how you plan to accept responsibility for it. Many times it is safer to call it a fiction and not worry about any charges of harming another person. Again, it is important for some people to set the record straight. They have a story to tell and have held it in long enough. After all, this is your story and from your point of view. The one person you have to be true to is yourself.

In building the foundation of your memoir, it is important to cover all of the major turning points you have had in your life first. Next, you need to edit the parts you don't want to share or come to grips with how you will disclose it. There will be times you are not sure of a certain point and this is where the research and fact checking are so important.

Part of the research you might want to do is interviewing others. It is always good to find out what you can first and have your questions ready. Remember if they learn you are writing a memoir or a novel based on your life, they may want to add their slant to the way things were. This is a good time to determine if they would love to be included or hate to have secrets disclosed. The internet is your friend; fact checking has never been easier. However, remember you can get sucked into it and never emerge. You have to decide when enough is enough and start working on the next step in authoring your memoirs or story based on your life.

In the writing of the memoir one important aspect is the way the facts or opinions are presented. It is one thing to present something as fact and another to say in your opinion. Be sure to let the reader know which it is and you will build credibility which is so very important.

EXERCISE 7
What are the major factual points you want to make in your memoir?

HOW TO WRITE YOUR MEMOIRS

Who are the people you need to check facts with?

_____
_____
_____
_____
_____
_____
_____
_____
_____
_____
_____
_____

If there is conflicting data, will you present both? If so, how do you plan on presenting both?

_____
_____
_____
_____
_____
_____
_____
_____
_____

Do you plan on writing your memoir as factual or fictional and how to you pan on letting the reader know which it is?

HOW TO WRITE YOUR MEMOIRS

_____
_____
_____
_____

What resources do you have at your disposal for research and which ones do you need to add?

DETERMINING THE AUTHOR'S VOICE AND POINT OF VIEW

Whose story is it any way? Many memoirs are told in first person giving them the feeling of a direct bond with the storyteller. But, it doesn't have to be. It could be told in third person as in a novel based upon a person's life. And, it could be told in second person with a close friends or narrator telling the story. To me this is perfect for a spouse telling the story of a deceased partner.
The story could be told in current time with reflection to memories in the past or start out in the past and read like that is the present time. Yes, many options and all different depending on the intent of the storyteller.

Many works today focus on an active voice that is strong and full of details. This gives the reader a more complete and accurate picture of what is happening. This is one section where it is okay to record your work in a passive voice and allow an experienced ghostwriter to polish for you.

Everyone speaks differently and everyone will tell a story in a different way. The voice of the storyteller carries a certain attitude and habits. Often it is referred to as the personality of the storyteller. No two people will tell a story the same way. It is this unique quality that draws a reader into a story. It is the one part of the story a gifted ghostwriter will work so hard in preserving.

Often during the interview section with the writer the voice will come out in the interviews. The method of writing and the way information is presented will also be discovered. A great ghostwriter wants to present the story in the storyteller's words.

Many great novelists know from experience they have to get out of the picture and let their characters tell the story. This is so much easier when you have an author telling the story. The objective is to get the reader connected to the storyteller. The less filters involved the better.

In deciding what voice to use the storyteller needs to think about the purpose behind the memoir. Is it to enlighten, amuse, or give words of wisdom? Making the voice a part of the story makes it more realistic and thus engaging. Many times the voice is not isolated and polished until later. This is fine since a memoir is polished many times as it is being developed. The voice has to be what the storyteller is comfortable in. Otherwise the story will come to a quick ending and the reader will never connect with it.

Some stories are easy to tell and others are painful, a different voice will help the author make it through these. In a life everyone experiences the good the bad and the ugly. Life is almost always about ups and downs. While the voice may take a while it will come. The best advice is to simply keep writing and learning what you are comfortable with. Remember without a first draft you will never have anything to polish.

EXERCISE 8
Which point of view do you plan to use in telling your memoir and why?

If you plan to use another person to tell your story, even if only for a short part of the memoir, who would that be and why?

Describe the tone you plan to use in your memoir. Is it to be a serious memoir or a comedy, etc.?

DETERMINING THE EXTENT THE BOOK IS FACTUAL OR FICTIONAL

It appears everyone wants to write his or her own memoirs lately. Memoirs have a range of truth to them that is assumed to be different by everyone. In looking for the truth in the memoir the degree imposed depends on many factors. A memoir is a slice of life written by someone who lived through the story. It is based on the memories and opinions of the memoirist. It is amazing to even think that ever item in such would be absolutely true.

The way the book is presented makes much of the difference. If the book is presented as accurate and the whole book or even parts of it are later discovered to be completed made up to deceive the reader is one thing, but honest mistakes are another. Again, if the writer is up front with the fact the book is a work of fiction inspired by a true life; the reader is prepared for the fictional part of the book. In truth, all books have elements of both in them. Even a science fiction or fantasy novel has elements of truth in them.

It takes some soul searching but worth the effort to determine what it is about your life that would make others interested in reading about it. First, a book written for your immediate family would be totally different from one written to be published and hopefully gain large royalties from. Inside jokes and experiences may make sense to your family but remain meaningless to others.

A famous person might be able to get away with telling their life without any special theme or meaning, but if you are not famous you need to discover what you have to say that will make others want to read about it. You need to express why your story is the story that must be told. Writing about grief or suffering is a great way to create closure or healing, but little to do with creating a best seller. A historical accounting of your life would be great to read to your grandchildren but not to others. The details of your daily life will never make interesting reading to the masses, but can be used to provide the background to a story. It is the story that sells the book. In specific, what is the hook in the book that grabs the reader?

Using the background and weaving a story is a skill that makes for a best seller. If you have all of the material together and need help writing the story itself, this is where a ghostwriter can help you the most. By saving the ghostwriter time in doing research and flushing out the story it will also save you money. To have a story you need motivation and conflict. It can be a combination of humor and suspense. However, it has to have emotional impact to move readers.

EXERCISE 9
Evaluate your position. Do you want to tell the truth and the whole truth or bend it in a fictional novel?

What are the points you think you need to talk to an attorney about for possible liable suits you maybe exposing yourself to?

Who are the characters you think might take offense to you exposing secrets? What do you think their reactions will be?

How do you plan to brace yourself for people's reaction to your frankness?

What are the events in your life you are hesitant in disclosing? How do you plan to make this decision?

What are your motivations for disclosing secrets you have?

WHAT IS THE PURPOSE OF TELLING THE STORY

Writing a memoir is a major project. Defining the purpose will give you more motivation to complete it. Having a clear statement will guide you along. Staying on track will remind you why you are spending so much time doing it.

One of the first reasons many people want to write a memoir is for the children and grandchildren. This can be a fantastic gift to them. It can preserve a legacy and give roots to your life and a blueprint to those who follow you.

Another reason is to write about the business you created from scratch. The future generation will want this to promote the business and to understand what went into the building of the company. If you spent a lifetime building a business that legacy needs to be preserved. No one but you will ever be able to do this.

We all become specialist in some field during our life. This information and wisdom needs to be preserved. This could be something as important as drugs or medical breakthroughs you invented to a recipe for grandmother's apple pie.

Many people have special events in their life. Many people in the future will want to know about these historical events. I would think someone for example caught in the world trade center bombing but managed to survive would have one heck of a story to preserve. But, it doesn't have to be that dramatic, only special and unique.

Also many people have obstacles they overcome in their life time. The story behind this can be fantastic reading. Everyone loves a rag to riches story or the comeback kid like Lance Armstrong for example. Remember again, it does not have to be this dramatic, only interesting enough to hook the reader and maintain their interest.

Most people have one special person in their life. A romance built into a memoir can be very powerful. I've often wondered why we don't see more true romance books which I think would be much more interesting than the predictable romances you see on the book stands. When love never gives up and finally triumphs, the world of readers will join you. The same is true when romance is not so happy ever after—divorce hurts—premature death devastates.

A memoir can have several subplots but the main

theme must be evident and the subplots must add to the story and not become a distraction. By delivering a compelling story your readers will want to read your memoir.
Reliving your life can unlock many memories that have been forgotten and secrets that now need to be disclosed, not to mention advice that others need to hear. Future generation can only learn from past mistakes if they are shared.

Everyone wants to have their life validated and to stand for something. Everyone placed on the planet is here for a reason and a purpose. Finding that purpose is what makes a good memoir. It is what makes writing the memoir so much easier. Another way to look at it is to determine what you consider interesting and your own motivation for writing the memoir. When these projects take on a life of its own you know you are on the right track. Allowing someone to live your inner thoughts and emotions pulls them into the story.

Many people think a memoir needs to written at the end of a life but a better memoir might be written as soon as a major event has happened to them. The details can be so much more fresh and relevant to the readers.

EXERCISE 10
What is your purpose for writing your memoir?

If there is a legacy you want to leave, what is it?

___

What is the main wisdom you want to pass on to your children or others?

What effect do you want your memoir to have on those who read it?

HOW TO WRITE YOUR MEMOIRS

What events in your life do you want to set the records straight on?

After all of these years what is the purpose for telling all now?

Some people write their memoirs to validate a life. What do you want people to take with them after they finish your memoir?

DETERMINING WHO IS THE INTENDED READER

By determining the purpose for writing the memoir this point is covered in a large degree but needs a slight elaboration. If the memoir is written only for your children to read and even then after your death, many family secrets can be revealed. There are no rules and you can follow any method or style you want.

If written for others to read and to publish for the world to understand your purpose brings on many new aspects. Deciding what family secrets to disclose or the tone you want to write can vary. How much truth and how much fiction you use will become important. Everyone wants to spice up their life. They want to show how they were the victim and not the villain in many cases. Many people want to set the record straight and thus the memoir might be targeted to certain people. You may have worked in a certain job and hated it forever or had a boss everyone thought was fantastic except those that know him well. Of course this brings up the question of legal liability.

The voice you use in your memoir can have slang if you want it only to be read by locals, but if you want it to be read by people all over, the slang might have to be tempered a bit. Determining who you hope will read your book is important in creating a perfect memoir to accomplish your purpose in doing so.

EXERCISE 11
Who specifically do you want to read your memoirs?

Who in general would benefit from the wisdom in your memoir?

_____

Who do you care less if they read your work?

Who would you like to dedicate your book to?

Who would you like to include in your memoirs?

If you plan to sell the book for mass distribution, which groups would these be best for?

JOHNNY RAY

HOW OPEN DOES THE MEMORIST WANT TO BE?

This varies from one person to another and needs to be addressed at some point. While many times in a person's life the memories are pleasant and fun to share there are other times when memoires can haunt and hurt as if it was happening all over again. Everyone will deal with this differently. Some will find it a way of healing and others a torture chamber. While working on the memoir this point will often shift many times and cause several rewrites. Remember it is your memoir and you are the author and get to decide what goes in and what stays out of your story.

Legalities also come to play in your story. You may know your neighbor as a thief but proving it might be hard to do in a court of law. Yes, the neighbor on the other side of you might sleep around, but try proving it when you get sued.

How you want to be remembered plays a role also in how open you want to be. Some of the events in your life you might not be so proud of. Everyone wants to be remembered in a good light. However, there may be someone you did wrong and have always wanted to apologize to. This might be the perfect opportunity to do so.

Remember also when you author a tell-all-book you open yourself to people telling secrets about you as well. Some events that might not seem important to you can be devastating to others. You might assume that everyone knew second cousin Joe was gay or your neighbor had an abortion, etc. But for them, keeping it a secret means everything to them.

The grand children might not ever know you were a party girl back in school 50 years ago. Would it be good to let them know? It might let them know they are not the only one who had problems, but it also might be a bad lesson for them and have them reject your values all together.
Consistency is important. The reader will know if you flip-flop on points and will soon learn to not trust you. However showing you are torn between two values or point of view can be good. This is where the story conflict comes in to play.

As an example say you lived with grandpa for a while before you married and later in life preach how bad it is that young people have no morals. Would you want to save your reputation or give advice? Would you want the world to know you had a struggle and conflict you overcome and lived with?

By telling what you wanted out of life and what

caused you to not have it sets up the story, the conflict that makes the memoir. By asking yourself what it was in life you really wanted and finally received answers many questions. Disclosing the details on how you obtained your goals requires some soul searching on how you might have taken short cuts or cheated a little here and there.

In a memoir as we discussed earlier, the accounting for the story can be factual or fictional. The degree one wants to be honest is up to them. The consequences of living with lies are up to the author. A lot depends on how it is presented to the reader. If it is sold as a tell-all memoir that accurately details a life it is expected to do so. If it is sold as a novel based upon a life it is received as being fictional. Revealing if real names are used or the names were changed will broadcast how the reader accepts the work.

Readers are happy with either method as long as it is presented honestly as to what they can expect. Readers of memoirs enjoy great writing as expected but look for more. They want to see inside the characters in the book and share their emotions, their victories and their agony in times of defeat. They want to feel the conflict. And unlike many books, they know the ending is unpredictable which is much different from a standard romance where you know everyone will live happy ever after. That is not always true in real life.

Many people hate to have their privacy invaded, especially when it is displayed in a bad light. Some people like celebrities and politicians have little defense since they chose to be in the public eye. Others have chosen a private life which is their right. For a reader secrets become very powerful in hooking their attention.

Determining how you will disclose certain issues will determine how you will add certain events to your memoir. Everyone has different taboo subject they will never touch. It could be sex, religion, politics or family. Some people want to shock their readers to set the record straight or get revenge from a previous fight, etc. Others want to hurt no one at any cost. As imagined the two will have totally different memoirs.

EXERCISE 12

Everyone wants to tell about their good times, their accomplishments and triumphs. How open do you think you can be about these events and make it sound like you are proud of them without sounding like you are bragging, etc.?

Everyone also has their share of failures and problems. How open do you plan to be on these events? Are you looking for sympathy or are you writing as a form of healing?

Being open can reveal secrets others in your family and friends do not want to disclose. How will this affect you as you write?

Being open can also subject you to lawsuits if you tell all and it affects others. Which events do you need to talk to an attorney about?

After your memoir comes out, some people might challenge you on your facts and opinions. How do you plan to deal with that?

SHOWING VERSES TELLING THE STORY

Showing versus telling is beat into a writers head daily as he works at his craft but totally alien to someone who is not a writer. Readers recognize it as good writing but have a hard time defining it. In its basic concept showing is giving all of the details of what is going on in a scene by showing what is happening and describing the details that enrich the experience of living through the scene. Telling is simply mentioning what is happening. Saying Joe was unhappy does not provide a lot of information. Whereas Joe sniffed back another tear then another before he lost control to the flood washing down his face gives a much stronger image of what is going on.

This is why it is so important to recall important details locked inside your memories. An author has the ability to recall important facts that the writer must have the ability to bring the story to life. Adding action and feeling to the scenes helps the reader to connect with the story.

When working on the basic outline of the memoir it is okay to skip past this important step so that the event can be recorded. But when time to write the scene, the all important details will be needed. This is the time to go back to those memoires and recall the reasons things happen. Everyone wants to hear a story and especially when they know all of the juicy details are included.

When an author summarizes by telling rather than dramatized using this showing technique the reader is unable to fell and envision the full impact of what is going on. Summarizing does not give the rich details that bring the reader into the story. The reader is being told what happened when the reader really wants to see and observe what happened.

There are some times when a summarization is necessary. Occasionally we do not need to get sidetracked into knowing a lot of details but only want enough to keep the main story on track. A combination of the two is needed in many cases to control the pace of the story. A story full of dramatic conversation will never give the reader time to reflect on what happen and is kind of like a James Bond movie on steroids.

While there are no rules that must be followed, the reader wants to engage the reader and hold his attention. In the process the author and writer will develop a unique voice the reader can expect and count on.

On the opening of any scene get to the action; the reader has to be hooked. Once hooked the pace has to retain the reader inside the story. Continue to ask yourself if there is anything I can make appear more vivid more real for the reader.

Another bad habit is to use the dialog to sneak in telling. It is just as bad. Telling one person something he should already know just to let the reader know always comes across as fake and unrealistic. The conversation has to be natural.

Allow the reader to be a witness to a real conversation. Let him see the scene in detail. Allow him to watch it as if in a movie. Let the actions and words of the characters show what is happening. In essences allow the characters to do their part and keep your author intrusions out of the story.
When a character slams down his plate because he hated the food, you don't have to add, he hated the food—the reader knows by the actions of the character. The best way to enforce and explain this is by using strong verbs that describe the actions. Mark Twain once said the difference between a word and the right word is the difference between a lighting bug and a bolt of lightning. Remembering this explanation always helps to work harder on finding that right word.

Readers want to feel, understand and be a part of the story. Give them the facts and they will make their own judgments and interpretations. Keeping the facts clear and the details full of rich descriptions will make the readers happy.

EXERCISE 13

This is something you need to do for each scene in your memoir, but for now we will concentrate on one scene. You might want to print out additional copies of this page for each scene in your memoir later.

Let us start with the most important scene in your memoir. Readers want details. What is the scene that you want to highlight the most?

_____
_____
_____
_____
_____
_____

First firmly plant the reader in this time and place. Is it early morning, late fall, perhaps Christmas time, etc.

_____
_____
_____
_____
_____
_____
_____
_____

HOW TO WRITE YOUR MEMOIRS

_____
_____
_____
_____
_____
_____
_____
_____

What are the smells you remember?

_____
_____
_____
_____
_____
_____
_____
_____
_____
_____
_____

What are the sounds you hear around you?

_____
_____
_____
_____
_____
_____
_____

Let your eyes roam around you and give vivid details of your surroundings.

HOW TO WRITE YOUR MEMOIRS

_____
_____
_____
_____
_____

Are you eating or drinking a beverage? How does it taste?

What are you feeling with your touch? Are you clothes comfortable or irritating? Are you cold?

Listing all of your sensory memories is important, but recording your inner thoughts adds the part most readers are interested in the most. What is going on in your head? Are you nervous or happy?

_____
_____
_____
_____
_____
_____
_____
_____
_____
_____
_____
_____
_____
_____
_____
_____
_____
_____
_____
_____
_____
_____
_____
_____

The reader wants to live your life with you. How else do you plan to make that happen?

Any time you feel like you are summarizing add details. Add actions. What is everyone doing in the scene? Think active verbs and bring the scene to life. What is everyone doing and be specific?

Sometimes after doing this exercise it is necessary to go back and do more research. Which items do you need to go back and research more?

HOW TO POLISH YOUR WORK

Once you have mastered a rough draft it is time to become ruthless. Much of what you wrote is not needed. It is best to start with the overall plot or theme of the work first before you waste time polishing line by line on sections that need to be thrown out all together.

Knowing what your overall theme and purpose for writing your memoir is helps so much and why we spent so much time on it in the beginning. However, knowing it has a way of coming back into the story, we need to address it again here. Every part of the book needs to build the story line and not distract from it. Background information is good to know but not needed in many cases in the story.

One of the first places to look is in the beginning of the book. So often the story really starts in chapter 3 or 5. If you still think this is important to the story, it may need to be added later in a flashback, etc.

The time table of the story needs to be reexamined. Is it consistent? Does it cover the slice of life you are presenting in the memoir? Does one part of the story flow logically from one section to the next or does it jump all over the place? Does every new chapter add to the conflict or the suspense of what is being told? Is the theme staying on target?

Are the characters growing? Are the readers learning more and more as layers of exposure are revealed? Are some characters introduced never to be heard from again? Do all of the characters maintain their own unique voice?

Once the basic structure is in place a closer look at the novel is in order. At the beginning of each chapter is a felling of setting given? Do we know who is there? Since the point of view can shift the reader needs to know whose eyes we are using to see the scene and hear the words spoken. Did the chapter flow smoothly from a previous chapter and follow a logical time period?

At the end of each chapter a hook needs to be added to keep the reader turning pages. This is used to build suspense or increase the tension that makes the story intriguing.

Studying the pace of the novel is important and can be difficult to evaluate by any author because the author knows what is coming next. This is the time to read the memoir as if you were the reader and pretend you do not know the rest of the story. If an author feels bored in any part you can bet the reader will feel the same way.

When the bases are covered on major points covered in the memoir, the work turns to line editing. Every word is looked at. Are passive words used? Are the verbs weak? Are the words spelled correctly—used correctly? Every writer also has certain words they repeat often and a list of these needs to be developed and checked for using the F1 function on the word processor.

Check for the over use of pronouns which give no clue as to what is being discussed or described. It went there gives us no idea as to what it is or where there is. Good writing is clear writing that the reader can follow.

EXERCISE 14
The first round of polishing is with the plot and theme itself. Restate your plot and purpose in writing the memoir.

List scenes or subplots that you think now might have to be eliminated.

Describe the opening in your memoir and why you think this is the best place to start.

Describe the middle of the book and what the conflict that is caring the book forward. What is the center makes the reader want to continue?

—

Is the ending appropriate for you memoir? Why do you think so? Did you accomplish your goal in writing the memoir here?

_____
_____
_____
_____
_____
_____
_____
_____
_____
_____
_____
_____
_____
_____
_____
_____
_____
_____
_____
_____
_____
_____
_____
_____
_____
_____

After getting all of the fundamental parts in line, polishing turns to fact checking. Are there items you need to go back and recheck? If so, which?

Polishing for grammar is fun for some people and not so for many. Make a list of those items you have problems with and recheck them by using the F1 key. This is just hard work and why many people want to hire a ghostwriter or an editor to polish their work. Still by going over and over your work it will get better. So, list the areas you need help with.

JOHNNY RAY

HOW TO FIND AN AGENT OR PUBLISHER

Getting your memoir published is the goal of many people. This way many people from around the world can hear your words of wisdom and your story and learn from you. First off, it is not easy to find either an agent or publisher if you do not have a track record or if you are not a celebrity or famous person with a large following or what is called a platform to generate sales.

But it is possible with the potential of making some fantastic money at it. Realizing that it is a lot of work and luck in the beginning helps to prepare you for what you are up against. When you enter the publishing world you are competing with the best writers in the world. Even if you had the work professionally written by a top ghostwriter you will still have battles in getting your story heard and purchased.

If you are famous and have a platform your story might be purchased on a proposal with the first three chapters completed. For all others, a completed work is needed. Most of the top publisher will not talk to a writer who is not presented by a literary agency. Getting an agent is also very hard.

Literary agents work on a percentage (usually 15%) of what the writer makes in royalties. They are flooded with writers wanting them to represent them and can afford to be very selective. Agents also specialize in what they handle. Finding the right one takes some research. A good place to start is http://www.agentquery.com. They all have different requirements on how they want to be approached. You will also see that many of them are closed to submissions.

Generally, to find an agent you have to submit a query letter which is a brief outline of what your book is about and ask them to look at the manuscript. Some agents also want a synopsis and some may even want opening pages. It is very wise to follow their instructions which they post on their web sites.

We will discuss the query letter, the synopsis and opening chapters in a few minutes. Many writers will tell you these are much harder to write than the memoir itself. Doing the research on how to write these perfectly is imperative.

The query letter has several parts that the agent will look for. It has to look professional and with some agents it is required in an e-mail and others it is required to be mailed to them. Again, follow their rules. Almost all require it to be on one page. This is what makes it tough.

Be sure to address the query to one specific person and get the name spelled correctly. Remember this is a professional business letter. Anything outlandish appears to be from an amateur and will receive an immediate rejection.

In the first line of the query state something personal about the agent so they know you are not sending this out to every agent in the country. If you meet the agent, let them know. If you did research which made you want to query them, let them know. If you can build their ego, do it. Again they want to know why you selected them. They want to know they are dealing with a professional.

The second paragraph is the reason for the query. An agent will want to know you have a finished memoir including what the word count is and the basic theme. A working title helps them to decide what they have to work with in trying to sell it. They want to know if what you have fits what they sell. Mentioning a previous work they sold helps if it is in the same vain as what you wrote.

All great memoirs have a hook. This has to be strong and to the point. It has to make the agent want to see more. It raises questions and generates excitement and intrigue. You have this one paragraph to sell your memoir.

The last paragraph is where you sell yourself. You tell of your platform and your writing abilities or that you hired a ghostwriter. Here, the agent wants to know if you can deliver a saleable product. They want to know if you have fans waiting in line to buy it and how you will promote it.
Finally, thank the agent for their time and consideration and that you look forward to their response. The hardest part is waiting for their response. Some will respond quickly, other will take forever.

According to the guidelines of the agent you might be able to submit a synopsis as well. For most agents this is usually around 3-5 pages where you can tell the major turning points of the memoir. This is not an outline and needs to be written in present tense. Here the agent is looking for writing skills and the ability to plot the story.

Other agents will ask for sample pages. Sample pages means the opening pages which could be as few as 4 or 5 and as many as 50 pages. It is important to have them properly formatted and grammatically correct. Here the agent is looking for writing ability and voice.

If you make it past this step you can expect a request for either a partial or full copy of the manuscript. A long wait time is now in order. You have to learn to be patient.
The happiest day in the life of any writer is the day you get the call. However, your work has only begun. Count on revisions and more polishing. When the agent offers you a contract, the book still has not sold; the agent has to find a buyer. It might take a while for her to obtain a publisher.

The name of the game is patience and polishing. After you polished your work, an agent will asks for polishing, the publisher will ask for more polishing and revisions. You can also receive request from copy editors and fact checkers.

Exercise 15
Take a trip to your local bookstore. Here go through the memoir section and see who is publishing the memoirs like you wrote. Usually at the front of the book, the author will thank their agent. What names did you see?

Go to agent query and add the names of agents that handle your type of memoir.

After coming up with your dream list of agents, start gathering information on them. The best place to start is their web site. Look for a way to make connection with them. Which conventions do they attend? What have they sold lately? You want to establish something you can use to let them know you selected them and why you picked them. Record your findings here.

_____
_____
_____
_____
_____
_____
_____
_____
_____
_____
_____
_____
_____
_____
_____

If you have not finished your memoir yet, you will have to wait until you do to query, but you can be reading the type of memoirs they handle to make sure your work fits what they like to sell. Which memoirs do you want to read from the list you have generated?

_____
_____
_____
_____
_____
_____
_____
_____
_____
_____
_____
_____
_____
_____
_____
_____

Work on a rough draft of your query letter, even if you have not started your memoir yet. The practice will serve you well. The most professional writers start with a goal in place. This will be yours. Yes, it will change many times, but worth the exercise.

HOW TO WRITE YOUR MEMOIRS

OTHER METHODS OF GETTING YOUR MEMOIRS PUBLISHED

The world of publishing has changed drastically lately. E-books are now out selling print books. Along with this change is the proliferation of smaller publisher. By searching online the names of these can be found and investigated.

Kindle is attempting to take over the world and offers an easy way to get your book published through them. In fact, it could be up and running in a matter of minutes. However, you may want to take a little more time to do so.
What you place on kindle is what you get. You receive no editing or critiquing. The errors you thought you caught and didn't will come back to haunt you. The mistakes you made in facts might land you in court.

However, hiring an editor or fact checker is not too expensive and can be worth the money. This way you have a final product you can be proud of. Even if you hired a professional ghostwriter I would still have it checked one more time. It will be worth it.

Kindle also does not do any advertising or promoting for you. Your book will be one of the millions on line. You will need to learn how to promote your memoir. The first step would be designing a cover page. Yes, there are people that do this for a living and worth their fees. The initial look at a book cover, even it is an e-book is important.

There are many book promoters out there also you need to make contact with. They can put you light years ahead of the competition. Since your book is an electronic book making the rounds of all of the social media sites on line is a must. Book blog tours are becoming the way to introduce your book. But don't forget old fashion promotions of TV and radio as well as print media of magazines and newspapers.

HOW TO HIRE A GHOSTWRITER
A ghostwriter can help you in many ways. They can be invisible and allow you to receive all of the credit or act as a partner or collaborator in the work. Some will handle every single detail and others will do only specific functions for you. Just as every story is different, every ghostwriter works differently.

Fist let us look at the difference between an author and the writer. The author is the one with the story that must be told. He or she has the information and the experiences to tell the story, but not the technical ability or craft to write. The writer on the other hand knows how to write but does not have the story or the experiences to write about.

Almost all ghostwriters work on a set fee which varies significantly as to cost. They usually are very happy to see someone else get the glory of the memoir. Knowing the amount of money they will make on royalties is a gamble and they would rather be writing than promoting a book, they want their money up front. Yes, some will work on a percentage of the royalties, but not many.

All ghostwriters will offer a contract that details what to expect and the prices to be charged. It is important to understand this contract. Both the author and the writer want this project to be completed as soon as possible but want it professional also.

When you consider hiring a ghostwriter to help you with your memoir, the cost has to be evaluated. A ghost writer can cost you from $5,000 for a short story to over $100,000 for a full length novel. So, what is it the ghostwriter will do for you to earn all of that money?

Obviously he will do the writing of the book, but he will usually do much more. Expect to be interviewed and questioned significantly as he probes for the story and background information. He will help bring facts and emotions out of you needed to make the story come alive. His job is to organize the story in a way that makes sense. He will help with the research and organize it as well. He can also help with deciding if a project is marketable. Pulling out the reason for the memoir is important to accomplish why you want to write the memoir.

Many people want to write a memoir but only a few actually do it. Time is a large part of the problem. Many people are busy with their own life and careers. A ghostwriter can save you a tremendous amount of time. Not only are they free to write but they are organized and efficient in what they do.

It is estimated that somewhere between 20,000 to over 100,000 works are written by ghostwriters every year. Of course, this number will never be known for sure. Many people recognize to get their work published they need help with their writing. It is very important to realize that a ghostwriter cannot guarantee your memoir will get published. It is the author's story and not the writers.
Many people want to write their life stories usually in the form of a memoirs and have visions of making lots of money or a perhaps seeing it in a movie. Time for a reality check—it probably is not

going to happen. The ghostwriter is not a magician. He will be able to improve your story and make sure it is written well, but the competition is enormous.

Does this mean you should not write your memoirs? Not at all! Your memoirs can obtain many other goals you set. And if getting your memoirs published is your goal, then by all means consider the services of a ghostwriter to give you ever advantage you can have. Just be sure to look at reality objectively.

With this as a background what should an author look for in a ghostwriter? Obviously someone with good writing skills would be a logical starting point. But digging deeper the personality and style of writing has to be considered. This is a person you will be spending a lot of time with and someone who will get very close to your deepest secrets.

Look for someone who will not force his own style on you but adjust to how you want to present the story.
If you are writing a memoir involving a business or specific industry you might want to find someone with some knowledge of the terms and feel of the landscape. Experience with similar books would be

a major plus. If publishing your book is a major goal then finding a ghostwriter with contacts in agencies and publishing houses is a big plus.

A ghostwriter will make different offers on what he can write a book for based on many factors. He is trying to guess how long it will take to write the book. The first consideration will be the length. A short story would only be around 3000 to 5000 words; a novella is usually around 15,000 to 30,000 words; a short novel around 50,000 words and a full novel close to 100,000 words.

He will want to know how much research has been completed and how much more he will have to do. Some research is easy and sometimes it can take a long time. Again, time is money. The ghostwriter could work by the hour, but many people are wary of this arrangement. The most common method is by the word or by the page. The contract will be based upon an estimate book size and adjusted later.

Most ghostwriter will want money up front before they begin to cover cost of getting started. While it varies, 25% is common. An additional 50% is due when the rough draft is finished. And the final 25% is due upon completion of the polished memoir. Along the way break clauses need to be added for the protection of the author and writer.

Many ghostwriter offer free consultation on your project and will only offer a contract after they have a feel for what they are obligating themselves for. Obtaining recommendations from ghostwriters is tricky since most times they are under contract not to disclose their involvement. This same consideration will be extended to you. Since you are making a major investment ask questions. Ghostwriter like answering questions and prefer to answer them now instead of later.

Establishing a time table for what has to be finished when takes coordination. Everyone has a busy schedule. If the author is still in the middle of a career and travels, etc. it might be hard to gather the information needed by the ghostwriter. On the other hand, if the ghostwriter is busy with many projects it could slow down the project. The ghostwriter might also be a full time novelist and working on his own material. All of this needs to be discussed and agreed to during the contract negotiations.

After the book is completed keeping the ghostwriter available for revisions and changes is critical. These you can count on from the various agents and editors who will be evaluating it. The process, even when you are a famous celebrity can take years.

Learn to be patient.

EXERCISE 17
Do you think you will use a ghostwriter? If so, what do you think would be the reason you need help?

Some ghostwriters offer a free consultation. What questions would you like to ask?

HOW TO WRITE YOUR MEMOIRS

What kind of budget do you have for a ghostwriter?

QUESTIONS A GHOSTWRITER WILL ASK YOU BEFORE STARTING

Everyone has filled out a questionnaire when they applied for a job. Yes, you know all of those intimate questions where they want to know everything about you. Guess what? Those questions were designed to give the employer facts about you. The ghostwriter will want much more. He will want to know your heart and soul and everything that makes you tick. Scary I know but necessary if the ghostwriter will write the book with the passion and intensity you want to express.

The ghostwriter will want to know why you want to hire him. It could range from not having the time or the skill to not really knowing why you want to write the book. The clearer you make your intentions to the ghostwriter the easier it will be for him to meet your goals. Also, without clear goals the ghostwriter might think you are wasting his time or worst think you will be one of those cases that will take more time than normal to write the book. The more time it takes him to write the book the more he will charge.

The ghostwriter will ask questions to ascertain the purpose of the book. Many times the memoirist knows his overall intentions but fails to express it.

When having to define the purpose the memoirist looks at his project in a whole new light. By thinking about this beforehand the time with the writer can be much more productive. Many ghostwriters have expertise in certain areas. If you intend to write a comedy out of your life with all of the funny events highlighted you might have the right ghostwriter and then you might not.

Each ghostwriter has a different style of writing like many artist and craftsman. Some will work with you intensely and stay in constant contact with you on every scene. Others will work hard to gather all of the information and disappear for a long time to create the story. Conversely, some memoirist want constant feedback on what the writer is doing and others want to be left along to do their job and advance their career until the work is finished and they can review it. Obviously for the project to be a success there has to be a connection of styles.

The writer will also want to know how much research has been completed and how much more will be needed. Is this a project you recently decided to take on or one you have considered for a long time? Bringing the ghostwriter up to speed is important for everyone. Having the ghostwriter do work you have already completed is not productive. Some of the story may already be written which is good and bad. The memoirist can expect much of it to be rewritten unless it has been polished and carefully plotted into the book. However by having some of the writing style of the memoirist the ghostwriter can easily adjust to bring out the memoirist true voice.

Eventually the talk will turn to money. While the memoirist is trying to understand what this will cost, the ghostwriter is trying to decide how much time will be involved in the project. Like any negotiation both are trying to get their best deal. The ghostwriter will often test the water by asking what kind of money the memoirist has budgeted for the project. And usually after letting the memoirist know roughly how much time this will take. The ghostwriter is thinking how much per hour or per day but will quote generally on a project bases. The normal price for a full length book is over $100,000 and a short story will be $5,000. However the price can be much more or less based on many circumstances.

Finally the time element comes into play. How long will it take to write the project? A clear understanding is important for both parties. The ghostwriter would like to have it completed as soon as possible but not so fast as to make the project a pain. Since the memoirist is paying most of the money upfront he would like to see the work as soon as possible also. Many times the ghostwriter has problems getting the information needed to complete the memoir. He wants to make sure he has access to the memoirist to answer questions and complete interviews on time.

After the final agreement to proceed is obtained a written contract needs to be entered into for both parties protection. This should cover all aspects of the agreement. If any part of the contract is not clear to you a competent lawyer should review the contract for you. It also helps to ask the other party for clarification.

The contract should naturally include the price to be paid for the work and how the price is calculated. The method of payment should be specified. Many ghostwriters will require an upfront fee which can vary from 25% to 50% in most cases. Some is due when the rough draft is finished and the final payment is due upon completion of the work.

Sometimes on a smaller work the entire fee is due upon signing. Since the writer is paid up front it is reasonable to expect to have time deadlines in the contract. Adjustments to the price need to be added for overruns, especially if caused by the memoirist in wanting to add additional material. Amendments to the contract will be added as needed.

Sometimes the ghostwriter will have expenses that need to be passed on to the memoirist for such items as supplies and travel expenses. Sometimes documents given to the ghostwriter are in a different language and need to be translated. In any case these expenses need to be agreed to upfront and included in the contract.

When the book is completed in most cases the ghostwriter is paid and has no further rights in the book will all royalties and payments from a publisher or buyer going directly to the memoirist. However, there can be exceptions. Giving the ghostwriter the right to add his name may result in a lower fee. There are many ways this can be accomplished and is an area where both parties need to negotiate if it is important to either side. The ghostwriter can be given credit by adding various words to show the involvement. The wording could indicate the ghostwriter assisted with the work, wrote part of it, edited it, or wrote the story based on memoirist telling the story to the ghostwriter. To the ghostwriter this is a business and he will weigh the value of all elements in the contract.

On a closing note, the ghostwriter is ascertaining if he wants to work with the memoirist as the memoirist is also trying to decide if the ghostwriter is someone he wants to work with. Due to the nature of a memoir the two will come to know each other very intimately. Is this the person you want to tell your most intimate secrets to? Can you trust this person completely to divulge things you have hidden from everyone all of your life?

Hopefully the process will go smoothly. The key is advanced preparation which is one of the main reasons for writing this book. By completing these worksheets the memoirist will be well on his way to having a great memoir writing experience. I wish you the best of luck to you and hope this guide and workbook help you.

EXERCISE 18

While this is a lot to consider it is now time to make an action plan and get busy. Use these remaining pages to plan your work. State your goals and live your dream of writing your memoir. You will always be glad you did. And remember to enjoy it.

_____
_____
_____
_____
_____
_____
_____
_____
_____
_____
_____
_____
_____
_____
_____
_____
_____
_____
_____
_____

HOW TO WRITE YOUR MEMOIRS

JOHNNY RAY

HOW TO WRITE YOUR MEMOIRS

www.ingramcontent.com/pod-product-compliance
Lightning Source LLC
Chambersburg PA
CBHW052033070526
44584CB00016B/2019